PLAY and LEARN

French

Ana Lomba *and* Marcela Summerville

Illustrated by Pedro Pérez del Solar
French Translation by Corinne Güngör
Audio Produced by Rob Zollman

McGraw·Hill

New York   Chicago   San Francisco   Lisbon   London   Madrid   Mexico City
Milan   New Delhi   San Juan   Seoul   Singapore   Sydney   Toronto

Library of Congress Cataloging-in-Publication Data

Lomba, Ana.
    Play and learn French / Ana Lomba and Marcela Summerville.
        p.   cm.
    ISBN 0-07-144151-4 (book and CD pkg.) — ISBN 0-07-144152-2 (book only)
        1. French language—Study and teaching (Preschool)—Activity programs.
    I. Summerville, Marcela.   II. Title

    PC2066.L66   2004
    372.654'1044—dc22   2004055163

*This book is dedicated to Ana's beloved daughter,
Marina Mulcahy, a special-needs child who
reminds us every day of the miracle of learning.*

3 4 5 6 7 8 9 0   CTP/CTP   0 9 8 7 6

ISBN 0-07-144151-4 (book and CD package)
ISBN 0-07-144152-2 (book only)

Interior artwork copyright © by Pedro Pérez del Solar
Interior design by Think Design Group LLC

McGraw-Hill books are available at special quantity discounts to use as premiums and
sales promotions, or for use in corporate training programs. For more information, please
write to the Director of Special Sales, Professional Publishing, McGraw-Hill, Two Penn
Plaza, New York, NY 10121-2298. Or contact your local bookstore.

Printed in China

This book is printed on acid-free paper.

Contents

Acknowledgments

We would like to express our heartfelt thanks and appreciation to the many friends and colleagues who have encouraged, supported, and believed in our work.

Specifically, we would like to thank the following people, who have facilitated book production and design:

- Pedro Pérez del Solar, illustrator, for his magical ability to bring our stories to life;

- Corinne Güngör, director of the Princeton French School, for bringing the French language and culture to the book;

- Rob Zollman, musician, who introduced us to the world of audiobooks and children's music;

- Bonnie Blader, our dear friend and unofficial proofreader, for her golden touch with language, adding flare to the English translation;

- Karen Young, our editor at McGraw-Hill, who guided us through the process of writing this book with keen insight and friendly advice.

We would also like to thank all those people in our personal lives who have made all this possible:

- Joseph, Victoria, Ana, Tyler, and Marina, our children, who have inspired the writing of our book;

- Ozzie Summerville and John Mulcahy, our husbands—we couldn't have done it without them;

- Our friends at the "French moms' group" for their unconditional help and support;

- The families in our classes, for being our best fans;

And, finally, we would like to thank the therapists, doctors, and nurses at home, at Princeton Medical Center, and at the Children's Hospital of Philadelphia who lovingly cared for little Marina Mulcahy. Special thanks to Dr. Utpal Shah, her pediatrician.

Introduction

If you want to open the world to your child, you first need to open your child to the world.

—Ana Lomba

Welcome to the world of early childhood language learning. Whether you are new to French or a native speaker, the language program presented in this book will help you effectively use your inherent skills as a "language teacher" in fun ways.

Regardless of your language knowledge and level, you have the skills needed to teach your child a second language. All parents teach their children a first language simply by using the language with them. All you need to do to teach your child a second language is to use the new language in the same way. We will provide you with all you need to get up and running: the how, what, when, and where.

This program shows you how to integrate French into your daily life. Because the activities in the program have been built around daily routines, you don't need to set a special time in your busy schedule. You will learn as you live.

Our Easy Immersion Methodology

Our program's methodology can be defined as "easy immersion," by which we mean using simple language constructions to describe obvious situations: "I'm drawing a circle," you may say while actually drawing a circle. Easy immersion is the natural way we speak to babies and young children. For example, while changing a diaper, you might say, "What a dirty diaper. Pew! Mommy is going to change it." Young children learn to communicate by modeling their caregivers' speech or sign language.

We believe that immersion is the most effective way to learn a language. Many language courses teach isolated words, but what can you do with them? Others teach commonly used expressions, but how can you continue the conversation? You need to learn whole language to be able to function in another language.

Our goal with the easy immersion methodology is to have you begin using whole French with your child today. With our program you don't need to learn grammar or to twist your tongue with difficult pronunciation exercises. All you need to do is use the activities provided to play with your child.

More and more studies show that early childhood is the best age to learn a language. Why delay? Get your child started early. This program is designed for children aged eighteen months to eight years.

How to Use This Book

Start with the activities most interesting to your child. This program isn't based on a linear progression. Begin with the activity you think your child will enjoy and proceed as you wish. Some situations are easier and others more complicated; thus the activities and conversations accommodate different ages and language levels.

Use the illustrations as a picture dictionary. Visual input will help strengthen understanding, accelerate oral fluency, and facilitate emerging literacy in the new language. Read the captions at the bottoms of the pages while pointing to the pictures, and then ask your child simple questions like *Laquelle est la fourchette?* (Which one is the fork?), *Où est le train?* (Where is the train?), or *Qu'est-ce que c'est?* (What is this?). Key French words and expressions (and their English counterparts) in the activities, games, and songs are **boldfaced** to facilitate learning and help build new vocabulary. Children's lines in song lyrics and responses in activities appear in *italics*.

Take it easy. We recommend taking baby steps. Don't try to learn everything at once. Follow your own child's learning rhythm. Start with the expressions or vocabulary words that you think will be most appealing to your child and then build by using the expressions in other situations as well.

Use the new language frequently.
Set your own goals and work at your own pace. Your child will benefit from as little as fifteen minutes of French three to four times a week. Please try to make these moments feel as natural and playful as possible and always follow your child's lead.

Don't let pronunciation stop you.
Traditional language learning programs put too much emphasis on pronunciation, which has proven counterproductive again and again. Your pronunciation will improve as you go. Our goal is to help you to communicate with all French speakers, not to speak with a perfect French accent. Your children will have an advantage over you in pronunciation, as their young minds will be able to register sounds to which you may have become deaf.

Make it a game. Your attitude is important. Young children respond better to exciting and playful endeavors than to formal "sit-and-recite" learning. Make learning French a game.

Don't hesitate to use the new language in front of French speakers. Why are you learning French if not to speak with native speakers? Chances are you and your child will make new friends and will enrich your knowledge of the new language and culture.

Expand the learning experience.
Consider creating a language corner for your child. The corner can include books, postcards, posters, and other culture-oriented items. If you have friends traveling to another country, ask them to bring you postcards, subway maps, menus, and other small souvenirs. Encourage your child to "teach" French to other family members. In this way you can build beyond the exercises in this book.

Focus on your interaction with your child. The best way to learn a language is through personal interaction. Tapes, videos, and other materials will help, but they will never be enough. That is why we encourage you to speak to your child in French. Never assume your child will effectively learn by simply parroting a tape or video.

Use the language naturally. Avoid constant translation and unnecessary explanations. If you translate to children, they will not make the effort to learn the new language. Use translation only if you see your child becoming frustrated.

Encourage but don't force speaking. Most children immersed in a second language pass through an initial "silent" period. While called "silent," it is not necessarily so, as children may respond in their first language. This is fine. Children need time to figure out the links between the new words and concepts, to understand, as well as to register and practice new sounds.

Don't be overly concerned about language "confusion." Mixing words, accents, and even grammatical structures is normal among young bilinguals. Contrary to common belief, this is not necessarily a sign of language confusion or of speech or language delay. Unfortunately, this common misunderstanding about language learning is the cause of much unnecessary sacrifice and suffering

for families who are advised to drop the second language. If you are concerned about your bilingual child's language development, seek the help of a therapist who specializes in bilingual issues, and educate yourself on the topic as well.

About the Language Used in This Book

One-on-one relationships. Our program focuses on one-on-one interaction to simplify learning and better respond to parental needs. While you will not learn plural verb forms at this point, learning them will be much easier and less confusing in the future. These activities can easily be adapted to teach a larger group of children by simply using the plural forms of the verbs.

One-way exchanges. In most situations, the parent is the only speaker. This is because children need a lot of input before they are able to speak, just as happens when parents speak to their children in their first language. Children begin producing utterances when they feel ready after hearing modeled speech.

Gender. In French, all nouns are either masculine or feminine. Because articles must agree in gender and number (i.e., singular or plural) with the noun they modify, it is a good idea to look at the article to determine if the noun is feminine or masculine. The masculine singular articles are "le" and "un" (*le garçon* = the boy; *un garçon* = a boy). The feminine singular articles are "la" and "une" (*la fille* = the girl; *une fille* = a girl). "L'" is used when the first letter of the word is a vowel or, sometimes, an "h" (*l'eau* = the water; *l'hôpital* = the hospital). "Du" or "de la" can also be used with singular nouns to indicate "some" (*du lait* = some milk; *de la salade* = some salad; *de l'eau* = some water). "Les" or "des" are used with plural nouns (*les fleurs* = the flowers; *des fleurs* = some flowers). Sometimes the articles "du," "de la," or "des" can indicate a general, all-encompassing meaning (*les bébés boivent du lait* = babies drink milk). Like articles, adjectives change gender and number as well. We have indicated differences in gender with slashes in the text (*belle/beau* = pretty/handsome).

We hope that you and your children enjoy hours of playing and learning together in French.

Bonjour!
Good Morning!

C'est l'heure de se lever!

Bonjour! C'est l'heure de se lever!
Réveille-toi, mon chéri. **Le soleil**
   est levé.
C'est l'heure de se lever! Bonjour!
Oh, **comme tu as sommeil**!
Réveille-toi, mon chéri.
Regarde, il fait jour. Le soleil est levé.
Soleil, petit soleil, réchauffe-moi,
Aujourd'hui et demain et toute
   la semaine.
Debout, paresseux!
Donne-moi ta main.
Oh, comme tu as sommeil!
Allez, on y va.
Fais attention aux **marches**.
Doucement. C'est ça.
Allons à **la cuisine**.
Qu'est-ce que tu aimerais pour ton
   petit déjeuner?

Time to Get Up!

Good morning! It's time to get up!
Wake up, honey. The **sun**
   is out.
It's time to get up! Good morning!
Oh, **how sleepy**!
Wake up, honey.
Look, it's daytime. The sun is out.
Sun, little sun, warm me up,
Today and tomorrow and all
   week long.
Up, lazy one!
Give me your hand.
Oh, how sleepy!
Come on, let's go.
Be careful with the **steps**.
Slowly. That's it.
Let's go to the **kitchen**.
What would you like for
   breakfast?

Did You Know?

In French, an adjective agrees in number and gender with the noun it describes.
For example: un sac vert *(masculine singular) becomes* des sacs verts
(masculine plural). Un navire bleu *(masculine singular), but* une valise bleue
(feminine singular) and des valises bleues *(feminine plural). The adding*
of an "e" to the end of an adjective generally indicates the feminine gender,
and adding an "s" indicates the plural form, although there are exceptions.

Le soleil

Comme tu as sommeil!

Les marches

La cuisine

6

C'est l'heure du petit déjeuner!

Time for Breakfast!

C'est l'heure du petit déjeuner.	It's time to have breakfast.
Aide-moi. Mettons la table.	Help me. Let's set the table.
Voilà **les céréales**. *Miam!*	Here is the **cereal**. *Yum!*
Voilà **le lait**.	Here is the **milk**.
Que nous faut-il d'autre?	What else do we need?
*Il faut **du jus d'orange**.*	*We need **orange juice**.*
Veux-tu du jus d'orange?	Do you want orange juice?
Voilà **les bols de céréales**.	Here are the **cereal bowls**.
Que nous faut-il d'autre?	What else do we need?
*Il nous faut **des cuillères**.*	*We need **spoons**.*
Que faut-il d'autre?	What else do we need?
*Il faut **des verres** pour le jus.*	*We need **glasses** for the juice.*
Voilà les verres pour le jus.	Here are glasses for the juice.
Lequel veux-tu, le vert ou le jaune?	Which one do you want, the green one or the yellow one?
Le vert.	*The green one.*
Très bien. Tout est prêt.	All right. Everything is ready.
Assieds-toi pour manger ton petit déjeuner.	Sit down to eat breakfast.
Oh, non! Tu as renversé le jus.	Oh, no! You spilled the juice.
Tiens, nettoie toi-même.	Here, clean yourself.

Le lait

Le bol

La cuillère

Le verre

Comme tu es belle/beau!

Avec de l'eau très propre,
*Mon **visage** je vais laver.*
Avec du dentifrice et une brosse à dents,
mes dents je vais laver.
Mets **le dentifrice** sur **la brosse**.
Brosse tes dents.
Lalalalalalalalala.
*Maintenant avec **le peigne**,*
*Je vais peigner mes **cheveux**.*
*Je me regarde dans **le miroir**.*
Ouah! Je vais être si belle/beau!
Ouah! Comme tu es belle/beau!

You Look So Beautiful/Handsome!

With very clean water,
*my **face** I will wash.*
With toothpaste and a toothbrush,
my teeth I will brush.
Put the **toothpaste** on the **toothbrush**.
Brush your teeth.
Chachachachachacha.
*Now with the **comb**,*
*I will comb my **hair**.*
*I look at myself in the **mirror**.*
Wow! I will look so pretty/handsome!
Wow! How pretty/handsome you look!

Did You Know?

Constantly correcting a person's language does not help in the language learning process. In fact, it actually interferes with it. A better way to help is to model. For example, if your child says, "Je suis froid" (using the verb être/to be when the expression requires the verb avoir/to have), just smile and say, "As-tu froid? Moi aussi, j'ai froid."

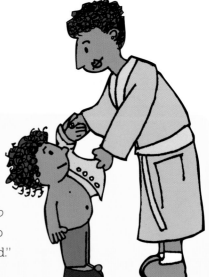

Le dentifrice

La brosse à dents

Le peigne

Le miroir

C'est l'heure de s'habiller!

Time to Get Dressed!

C'est l'heure de s'habiller!
Regardons dans l'armoire.
Voyons—**des pantalons, des jupes,
Des chemisiers, des t-shirts...**
Qu'est-ce que tu veux mettre?
Veux-tu la jupe rouge?
Ce pantalon?
Ce t-shirt vert
ou le chemisier jaune?
Le jaune.
Très bien. Enfile **un bras**.
Enfile l'autre bras.
Passe **la tête**. Ça y est!
Et quoi d'autre? Ce **short**?
Bien. Tiens-toi à moi.
Enfile **une jambe**.
Enfile l'autre jambe.
Ça y est!
Ouah, comme tu es jolie!

Time to get dressed!
Let's look in the closet.
Let's see—**pants, skirts,
shirts, T-shirts . . .**
What do you want to put on?
Do you want the red skirt?
These pants?
The green T-shirt
or the yellow shirt?
The yellow one.
Very good. Put in your **arm**.
Put in your other arm.
Put in your **head**. All done!
And what else? The **shorts**?
Good. Hold on to me.
Put in your **leg**.
Put in your other leg.
All done!
Wow, how nice you look!

Un pantalon

Une jupe

Un t-shirt

Un short

Allons dehors!
Let's Go Outside!

Il fait froid!
Il fait chaud!

It's Cold! It's Hot!

Voyons quel temps il fait aujourd'hui.
Ah! Il fait si froid! Comme il fait froid!
Il fait très froid! Il fait très froid!
Je mets mon **chandail** car il fait
    très froid.
Il fait très froid! Il fait très froid!
Je mets mon **bonnet** car il fait
    très froid.
Il fait très froid! Il fait très froid!
Je mets ma **veste**.
Je mets mes **gants**.
Je mets mon **écharpe**.

Rentrons maintenant. Ah!
    Il fait très chaud!
Il fait très chaud! Il fait très chaud!
J'enlève ma veste car il fait très chaud.
Il fait très chaud! Il fait très chaud!
J'enlève mon écharpe car
    il fait très chaud.
J'enlève mes gants.
J'enlève mon bonnet.
J'enlève mon chandail.

Let's see what the weather is like today.
Aah! It's so cold! How cold it is!
It's very cold! It's very cold!
I put on my **sweater** because it's
    very cold.
It's very cold! It's very cold!
I put on my **hat** because it's
    very cold.
It's very cold! It's very cold!
I put on my **jacket**.
I put on my **gloves**.
I put on my **scarf**.

Let's go inside now. Aah!
    It is very hot!
It's very hot! It's very hot!
I take off my jacket because it's very hot.
It's very hot! It's very hot!
I take off my scarf because
    it's very hot.
I take off my gloves.
I take off my hat.
I take off my sweater.

Un bonnet

La veste

Une paire de gants

Une écharpe

La souris et les chaussures

The Mouse and the Shoes

Allez, nous devons partir!	Come on, we have to go!
Où sont tes chaussures?	Where are your shoes?
Chaussures, où êtes-vous?	Shoes, where are you?
Elles doivent être avec la souris.	They must be with the mouse.
Une souris, souris, souris,	A mouse, mouse, mouse,
est montée dans	went up
une chaussure marron.	a **brown shoe**.
La chaussure a fait tap, tap,	The shoe went tap, tap,
et la souris a roulé, roulé.	and the mouse rolled, rolled.
Une souris, souris, souris,	A mouse, mouse, mouse,
est montée dans **une chaussure bleue**.	went up a **blue shoe**.
La chaussure a fait tap, tap,	The shoe went tap, tap,
et la souris a roulé, roulé.	and the mouse rolled, rolled.
Est montée dans **une chaussure noire**.	Went up a **black shoe**.
Est montée dans	Went up
une chaussure blanche.	a **white shoe**.
Allez, nous devons partir!	Come on, we have to go!
Mets tes chaussures. Noue tes lacets.	Put on your shoes. Tie your shoelaces.
Oh, non! Voilà la souris!	Oh, no! Here comes the mouse!
Cours, cours! La souris arrive!	Run, run! The mouse is coming!

Une chaussure marron   Une chaussure bleue   Une chaussure noire   Une chaussure blanche

Cuisinons!
Let's Cook!

Au supermarché

Nous allons au supermarché.
Veux-tu monter dans **le chariot**?
Voilà la liste.
Nous avons besoin de deux
    poivrons verts.
Voilà, un et deux. *Deux poivrons verts.*
Mets-les dans le chariot.
C'est fait.
Maintenant, nous avons besoin de
    trois **oignons**.
Voilà, un, deux et trois. *Trois oignons.*
Mets-les dans le chariot.
C'est fait.
Quoi d'autre?
Il nous faut **de l'ail**.
Voilà, une tête d'ail.
Mets-le dans le chariot.
C'est fait.
Maintenant, il nous faut **du pain**.
Voilà, du pain.
Mets-le dans le chariot.
C'est fait.
Du beurre, du yaourt et **des œufs**.
Mets-les dans le chariot.
C'est tout. Allons payer.

Let's Go to the Supermarket

We're going to the supermarket.
Would you like to go in the **cart**?
Here's the list.
We need two
    green peppers.
Here, one and two. *Two green peppers.*
Put them in the cart.
It's already there.
Now, we need
    three **onions**.
Here, one, two, and three. *Three onions.*
Put them in the cart.
It's already there.
What else?
We need **garlic**.
Here, a head of garlic.
Put it in the cart.
It's already there.
Now, we need **bread**.
Here, bread.
Put it in the cart.
It's already there.
Butter, yogurt, and **eggs**.
Put them in the cart.
That's all. Let's pay.

Un poivron vert

Un oignon

Une tête d'ail

Des œufs

Cuisinons ensemble

Veux-tu m'aider à cuisiner?
Nous allons faire une ratatouille.
  Miam!
D'abord il faut laver les poivrons.
Voilà, lave-les.
Maintenant nous devons les ouvrir.
Enlève **les pépins**. Bien.
Coupe-les en petits morceaux,
  comme ça.
Maintenant lavons **les tomates** et
  les courgettes.
Essuie-les. Bien.
Coupe les tomates avec
  un couteau en plastique.
En petits carrés, comme ça.
Coupe les courgettes en petits carrés.
Et maintenant, faisons-les cuire!
Mets **de l'huile** dans **la poêle**.

Let's Cook Together

Will you help me cook?
We are going to make ratatouille.
  Yummy!
First we need to wash the peppers.
Here, wash them.
Now we have to open them up.
Take out the **seeds**. Good.
Cut them in small pieces,
  like this.
Now let's wash the **tomatoes** and
  the **zucchini**.
Dry them. Good.
Cut the tomatoes with
  a plastic knife.
In little squares, like this.
Cut the zucchini into little squares.
And now, let's fry them!
Put **oil** in the **pan**.

Did You Know?

Ratatouille *is a common dish in southern France. Eggplant, squash, peppers, onions, and tomatoes are sautéed in olive oil. Add salt and pepper and cook.*

Une tomate

Une courgette

Une bouteille d'huile

Une poêle

L'heure du déjeuner
Lunchtime

Le déjeuner

Lunch

C'est l'heure de manger!
Qu'est-ce qu'il y a à déjeuner?
De la soupe et **du poisson**.
Je n'ai pas faim.
Mais tu dois manger un petit peu.
Je n'ai pas faim.
Voilà, la soupe. Goûte-la. Seulement un
petit peu.
C'est quoi ce truc orange?
C'est **de la carotte**.
Je n'aime pas les carottes.
Et c'est quoi ce truc vert?
Ce sont **des petits pois**.
Je n'aime pas les petits pois!
C'est quoi ce truc marron?
C'est **de la viande**.
Je n'ai pas faim.
Il y a aussi **de la glace**.
Je veux de la glace! Ça j'aime!
Je croyais que tu n'avais pas faim!
Mange un petit peu de soupe et
de poisson et je te donnerai de la glace.

Time to eat!
What's for lunch?
Soup and **fish**.
I'm not hungry.
But you have to eat a little.
I'm not hungry.
Here, the soup. Try it. Only a
little bit.
What is this orange stuff?
They're **carrots**.
I don't like carrots.
And what is this green stuff?
They're **peas**.
I don't like peas!
What is this brown stuff?
It's **meat**.
I'm not hungry.
There's also **ice cream**.
I want ice cream! That I like!
I thought you weren't hungry!
Eat a little bit of soup and
fish and I'll give you ice cream.

Did You Know?

In France, lunch has always been an important meal. It is a time for good conversation as well as good food. Taking more than an hour for lunch is not unusual. In schools, for example, classes may stop at 11:30 A.M. and reconvene at 1:30 P.M. Some children go home for lunch, and many small shops close during lunchtime so the owners can go home to eat with their families.

Des carottes

Des petits pois

De la viande

De la glace

La soupe folle

Crazy Soup

**La nappe, les bols, les assiettes,
la soupe, la grande cuillère**
—C'est prêt!
C'est l'heure de manger!
Chez mon oncle,
ils mangent la soupe avec **un couteau**.
Qu'est-ce que tu fais?
Manges-tu ta soupe avec un couteau?
Ah, là, là! Tu es fou!
Ah, là, là! Quelle drôle de chose!
Chez Raymond,
ils mangent la soupe avec
une fourchette.
Qu'est-ce que tu fais?
Manges-tu ta soupe avec
une fourchette?
Ah, là, là! Tu es fou!
Ah, là, là! Quelle drôle de chose!
Chez ma sœur,
ils mangent la soupe avec **une cuillère**.
C'est bien! Une cuillère!
Ah, là, là! Comme c'est bon!
Ah, là, là! J'en veux encore un peu!
Encore de la soupe, s'il te plaît!

**Tablecloth, bowls, plates,
soup, big spoon**
—All set!
Time to eat!
In my uncle's house,
they eat soup with a **knife**.
What are you doing?
Do you eat your soup with a knife?
Ay, ay! How crazy you are!
Ay, ay! What a foolish thing!
In Raymond's house,
they eat soup with
a **fork**.
What are you doing?
Do you eat your soup with
a fork?
Ay, ay! How crazy you are!
Ay, ay! What a foolish thing!
In my sister's house,
they eat soup with a **spoon**.
Good thing! A spoon!
Ay, ay! How tasty it is!
Ay, ay! I want a little bit more!
More soup, please!

Une nappe

Un bol

Une assiette

Une grande cuillère

L'heure du dîner
Dinnertime

Révolution dans la cuisine!

Ah, là, là, que se passe-t-il dans
  la cuisine
pour qu'il y ait une telle révolution?
Le faitout crie et crie
que le dîner est prêt,
et que la table n'est pas mise.
Le plat est arrivé en roulant
pour s'asseoir à table
et il a eu la grande surprise
de voir qu'il n'y avait pas de nappe.
Très effrayé, **le verre** a crié:
Je suis pour l'eau, pas pour la soupe!
La louche, très imbue d'elle-même,
a dit à l'assiette à soupe:
Viens, je vais te servir la soupe
puisque tu n'es pas un verre.
Manger la soupe m'est pas facile si c'est
avec **une fourchette** ou **un couteau**.
Mange la soupe avec **une cuillère**,
ainsi tu ne te saliras pas la figure.
La corbeille à pain très effrayée a crié:
Je me suis salie avec **un cracker**!
Voilà, je viens t'aider!
—a dit **la serviette en papier**.
Silence!—a crié **le sel**—
cette révolution doit cesser;
c'est l'heure de dîner.

Revolution in the Kitchen!

Ay, what happens in
  the kitchen
that there is such a revolution?
The **pot** screams and screams
that dinner is ready,
and the table is not set.
The **dish** arrived rolling
to sit at the table
and it had a big surprise
to see that there was no tablecloth.
Very scared, the **cup** screamed:
I am for water, not for soup!
The **ladle**, very huffy,
told the soup dish:
Come, I will serve you the soup,
since you are not a cup.
Eating soup with a **fork**
and a **knife** is not simple.
Eat soup with a **spoon**,
that way you won't get your face dirty.
Terrified, the **breadbasket** screamed:
I got dirty with a **cracker**!
Here, I will help you!
—said the **napkin**.
Silence!—screamed the **salt**—
this revolution must come to an end;
it is dinnertime.

Un faitout

Un verre

Une corbeille à pain

Un cracker

16

Le dîner

Dinner

C'est l'heure de dîner!
Le dîner est prêt! Passons à **table**!
Il y a **du rôti**
avec **de la purée de pommes de terre**
    et **de la salade**.
As-tu soif?
Voilà un verre **de lait**.
Bois-le doucement.
As-tu faim?
Voilà un peu **de pain avec du beurre**.
Donne-moi ton assiette, s'il te plaît.
Un morceau de viande, un petit peu
    de purée de pommes de terre,
et un peu de salade.
As-tu besoin d'un couteau pour couper
    la viande?
Tiens, mais fais attention,
    ne te coupe pas.
Si tu termines tout, mais vraiment tout,
je te donnerai **des fraises avec
    de la crème**.

It is dinnertime!
Dinner is ready! Let's sit at the **table**!
There is **roasted meat**
with **mashed potatoes**
    and **salad**.
Are you thirsty?
Here's a glass of **milk**.
Drink it slowly.
Are you hungry?
Here is a little **bread with butter**.
Give me your plate, please.
A piece of meat, a little bit
    of mashed potatoes,
and a little salad.
Do you need a knife to cut
    the meat?
Here, but be careful,
    don't cut yourself.
If you finish it all, and I mean all,
I'll give you **strawberries with
    cream**.

Du rôti

De la purée de pommes
de terre

Une salade

Les fraises avec
de la crème

Dans la cuisine
In the Kitchen

Le dessert

Dessert

Que veux-tu comme **dessert**?

Il y a **des mandarines, des poires, des raisins** et **des bananes**.

Aimerais-tu une mandarine?

Oui, une mandarine.

Épluchons-la.

Enfonce ton ongle.

Comme ça. Regarde comment je fais.

Maintenant, retire **la peau** comme ça.

Sépare **les quartiers**.

*Il y a **des pépins**.*

Retire-les avec ton ongle.

C'est si juteux.

Voilà une serviette en papier.

What do you want for **dessert**?

We have **tangerines, pears, grapes,** and **bananas**.

Would you like a tangerine?

Yes, a tangerine.

Let's peel it.

Stick your nail in.

Like this. Look how I do it.

Now, pull back the **skin** like this.

Separate the **slices**.

*It has **seeds**.*

Take them out with your nail.

It's so juicy.

Here's a napkin.

Did You Know?

Fruit is often eaten at the end of a French meal, and fruit and yogurt are often given to children as dessert. Of course, the fruits offered change with the seasons. Other desserts, such as pastries, are also eaten from time to time. Water and wine are the main drinks served with French meals. After dessert, adults might also have a cup of coffee or an herb infusion, but these are never served during the meal. The coffee is strong and served in small cups (like espresso).

Une mandarine

Une poire

Des raisins

Une banane

Nettoyons la cuisine — ## Let's Clean the Kitchen

La cuisine est tellement sale!
  Nettoyons-la.
Il faut mettre les assiettes dans
  le lave-vaisselle.
Les assiettes vont en bas.
Les verres vont en haut.
Les couverts vont dans le panier.
Nous devons nettoyer **la table**.
Voilà la lavette. Nettoie la table.
Le sol est tellement sale!
Nettoyons-le.
Tiens, **le balai**.
Balaie le sol.
Voilà **la pelle** pour les saletés.
C'est encore sale.
Maintenant, nous devons laver le sol.
Voilà **la serpillère**.
Lave le sol.

The kitchen is so dirty!
  Let's clean it up.
We need to put the plates in
  the **dishwasher**.
The plates go down here.
The cups go up here.
Silverware goes in the basket.
We have to clean the **table**.
Here's the dishcloth. Clean the table.
The **floor** is so dirty!
Let's clean it.
Here, the **broom**.
Sweep the floor.
Here's the **dustpan** for the trash.
It's still dirty.
Now, we have to mop the floor.
Here's the **mop**.
Mop the floor.

Un lave-vaisselle

Un balai

Une pelle

Une serpillère

L'heure du bain!
Bath Time!

À l'eau, canard!

C'est l'heure du bain!
La baignoire est remplie
    d'eau chaude.
Laisse-moi t'aider à enlever tes
    vêtements.
Un, deux et trois. Prêt!
À l'eau canard! Couac, couac, couac.
Ne me mouille pas!
C'est l'heure de baigner ce **caneton**.
Ferme tes **yeux**, je vais verser
    de l'eau sur toi.
Un petit peu **de shampooing** pour
    tes cheveux.
Je gratte, gratte, gratte.
N'ouvre pas tes yeux encore.
Les cheveux sont propres.
Avec quoi vais-je laver mon caneton?
Voilà **une éponge** et **un savon**.
Je lave tes **mains**.
Je lave ta petite **figure**.
Je nettoie ton **nez**. Miam! Je l'ai mangé!
Comme mon caneton est propre!
Avec quoi vais-je sécher mon caneton?
Avec cette **serviette** douce, douce.

Duck, to the Water!

It's bath time!
The **bathtub** is filled with
    warm water.
Let me help you take off your
    clothes.
One, two, and three. Ready!
Duck, to the water! Quack, quack, quack.
Don't get me wet!
It's time to bathe this **duckling**.
Close your **eyes**, I'm going to pour
    water on you.
A little bit of **shampoo** for
    your hair.
I scratch, scratch, scratch.
Don't open your eyes yet.
Clean hair.
With what do I wash my duckling?
Here is the **sponge** and here is the **soap**.
I wash your **hands**.
I wash your little **face**.
I wash your **nose**. Yum! I ate it!
How clean my duckling is!
What do I dry my duckling with?
With this soft, soft **towel**.

Did You Know?

Bath time is a great opportunity to teach your child the names of body parts. You may want to expand this activity by having your child bathe a doll. Model the behavior and encourage your child to take care of his or her "child" using French words.

La baignoire

Un caneton

Le shampooing

L'éponge

Une serviette, une éponge et du savon

Towel, Sponge, and Soap

Cette chanson est chantée avec
    une serviette, une éponge et du savon.
Nous tirons **le rideau de douche**…
Nous ouvrons **le robinet**…
À l'eau, mon trésor!
Comme ça, comme ça, comme ça,
comme ça je lave mes cheveux.
Comme ça, comme ça, comme ça,
je les ai déjà lavés.
Comme ça, comme ça, comme ça,
comme ça je lave mes mains.
Comme ça, comme ça, comme ça,
je les ai déjà lavées.
Comme ça, comme ça, comme ça,
comme ça je rince ma figure.
Comme ça, comme ça, comme ça,
je l'ai déjà rincée.
Comme ça, comme ça, comme ça,
comme ça j'éclabousse.
Comme ça, comme ça, comme ça.
Oh! J'ai fait une petite flaque.
Sors de l'eau, mon trésor.
Viens et sèche-toi avec cette **serviette**.

This song is sung with
    towel, sponge, and soap.
We open the **shower curtain** . . .
We turn on the **faucet** . . .
Into the water, honey!
Like this, like this, like this,
like this I wash my hair.
Like this, like this, like this,
I already washed it.
Like this, like this, like this,
like this I wash my hands.
Like this, like this, like this,
I already washed them.
Like this, like this, like this,
like this I rinse my face.
Like this, like this, like this,
I already rinsed it.
Like this, like this, like this,
like this I splash water.
Like this, like this, like this.
Oh! I made a little puddle.
Get out of the water, honey.
Come and dry yourself with this **towel**.

Le savon

Le rideau de douche

Le robinet

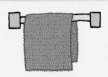

La serviette

Bonne nuit!

Good Night!

Au lit!

Allons dans ta **chambre**.
Trouvons **un pyjama** propre.
Mais d'abord
    un sous-vêtement propre.
Tiens, mets ce sous-vêtement.
D'abord un pied et puis l'autre pied.
Tiens, mets ce pyjama.
D'abord la tête, puis les bras.
Maintenant **le pantalon**.
D'abord une jambe et puis l'autre.
Va dans la salle de bains et brosse-toi
    les dents.
Brosse-les bien, en haut et en bas.
As-tu fait pipi? Non?
Fais pipi alors.
Fais-moi un bisou pour la nuit
et va au **lit**.
Prends ton **nounours** et grimpe
    dans ton lit.
Je vais te couvrir.
Nous allons lire cette **histoire**.
Il était une fois une lune
qui ne voulait pas dormir…

Let's Go to Bed!

Let's go to your **bedroom**.
Let's find clean **pajamas**.
But first
    clean **underpants**.
Here, put on these underpants.
First one foot and then the other foot.
Here, put on these pajamas.
First your head, then your arms.
Now the **pants**.
First one leg and then the other.
Go to the bathroom and brush your
    teeth.
Brush them well, up and down.
Have you made pee pee? No?
Make pee pee then.
Give me good-night kisses
and go to **bed**.
Take your **teddy bear** and get
    in bed.
Now I'll cover you.
We're going to read this **story**.
Once upon a time there was a moon
that didn't want to sleep . . .

Did You Know?

Reading foreign language books to your child three or more times a week is an excellent way to help him or her understand and develop new vocabulary. At first, choose picture books that use repetition, rhyme, and limited vocabulary. Then use the words and expressions learned in real-life conversation.

Une chambre

Un pyjama

Un sous-vêtement

Le lit

La lune

La lune, la lune
sortit pour une promenade,
par une belle **nuit** claire
avec sa nouvelle robe.
Elle se regarda dans un étang.
Elle vit qu'elle était belle.
Elle peignit ses lèvres
en rose.
Cette nuit-là, elle invita **une étoile**
à se promener,
mais l'étoile lui dit:
Seulement si c'est en voiture.
Elle invita **le soleil**,
mais le soleil ne voulut pas,
car il ne pouvait
sortir que le jour.
La lune, la lune,
seule et s'ennuyant,
mit son pyjama
et s'endormit.

The Moon

The **moon**, the moon
went out for a walk,
on a clear **night**
with her new dress on.
She looked at herself in a pond.
She saw she was beautiful.
She painted her lips
with the color pink.
That night, she invited a **star**
to go out for a walk,
but the star told her:
Only if it is by car.
She invited the **sun**,
but the sun didn't want to,
because he could only
come out during the day.
The moon, the moon,
alone and bored,
put on her pajamas
and fell asleep.

La lune

La nuit

Une étoile

Le soleil

L'heure de jouer!
Playtime!

À cache-cache

Hide-and-Seek

Jouons à cache-cache.
Je vais cacher ton petit chien.
Tu fermes les yeux et tu comptes.
Un, deux, trois, quatre, cinq, six, sept,
huit, neuf et dix.
Ouvre les yeux!
Cherchons le petit chien.
Petit chien, où es-tu?
Où es-tu, petit chien?
"Ouaf, ouaf". Je l'entends!
Serait-il derrière **le rideau**?
Non, il n'est pas là.
Serait-il sous **la table**?
Non, il n'est pas là.
Serait-il derrière **le canapé**?
Non, il n'est pas là.
Je sais! Serait-il dans **le tiroir**?
Oui, il est là!
Maintenant tu te caches et je compte.

Let's play hide-and-seek.
I'm going to hide your doggy.
You close your eyes and count.
One, two, three, four, five, six, seven,
eight, nine, and ten.
Open your eyes!
Let's look for the doggy.
Doggy, where are you?
Where are you, doggy?
"Bow wow, bow wow." I hear him!
Could he be behind the **curtain**?
No, he's not here.
Could he be under the **table**?
No, he's not here.
Maybe he's behind the **sofa**?
No, he's not here.
I know! Will he be inside the **drawer**?
Yes, he is here!
Now you hide and I will count.

Did You Know?

There are more bilingual than monolingual people in the world.
A popular belief in monolingual countries is that the brain can
only deal with one language, but research has shown that this is
not the case. Quite the contrary, learning languages helps exercise
the brain and build thinking and cultural flexibility. The quality
of the education received is the key to success in any language.

Un rideau

Une table

Un canapé

Un tiroir

Rangeons

Let's Put It Away

Note: Repeat the *refrain*/chorus after every other object that needs to be put away.

Refrain:	**Chorus:**
Nous allons ranger.	We're going to put things away.
Quel désordre!	What a mess!
Nous allons ranger ta	We're going to clean your
chambre maintenant.	room now.
Nous allons ranger.	We're going to put things away.
Quel désordre!	What a mess!
Nous allons ranger ta chambre.	We're going to clean your bedroom.
Ouah! Quel désordre!	Yikes! What a mess!
Nous allons ranger.	We are going to put things away.
*Où vont **les poupées**?*	*Where do the **dolls** go?*
Les poupées vont sur le lit.	The dolls go on the bed.
***Les soldats**?*	*The **soldiers**?*
Les soldats dans la boîte. *(Refrain)*	The soldiers in the box. *(Chorus)*
***Les camions**?*	*The **trucks**?*
Nous devons garer les camions.	The trucks we have to park.
***La nourriture**?*	*The **food**?*
La nourriture va dans la cuisine. *(Refrain)*	The food goes in the kitchen. *(Chorus)*
***Les costumes**?*	*The **costumes**?*
Les costumes dans la penderie.	The costumes in the closet.
***Le râteau**?*	*The **rake**?*
Que fait le râteau ici?	What is the rake doing here?

Les poupées

Les soldats

De la nourriture

Les costumes

Jouons aux pompiers!
Let's Be Firemen!

Jouons aux pompiers

L'alarme sonne! L'alarme sonne!
Dépêche-toi! Dépêche-toi!
Maintenant, descendons **la perche**.
Mets ta **combinaison**.
Mets tes **bottes**.
Et maintenant ton **casque**.
Monte dans le camion. *Prêt?*
Dégagez la route! *Dégagez la route!*
Déclenche **la sirène**.
Éteignons ce **feu**!
Prends **le tuyau**.
Envoie **l'eau**.
Monte! Monte à l'échelle!
Plus d'eau! *Plus d'eau!*
Excellent travail!
Le feu est éteint.

Playing Firemen

The alarm is ringing! The alarm is ringing!
Hurry! Hurry!
Now, let's go down the **pole**.
Put on your **suit**.
Put on your **boots**.
And now your **helmet**.
Get in the truck. *Ready?*
Clear the way! *Clear the way!*
Turn on the **siren**.
Let's put out the **fire**!
Grab the **hose**.
Blast the **water**.
Up! Climb up the ladder!
More water! *More water!*
Great job!
The **fire** is out.

Did You Know?

You can make a fire truck with a large box. Use big paper plates for the wheels and small ones for the headlights and the siren. Make a hose with a vacuum-cleaner hose or a piece of water hose. Your child can wear a big bowl as a helmet, snow boots, and a big yellow or red shirt for the uniform.

Un pompier

Un casque de pompier

Un tuyau

Un jet d'eau

Le camion de pompiers

The Fire Truck

Dépêche-toi! *Dépêche-toi!*
Allons-y! Allons-y maintenant!
Allons-y! Allons-y maintenant!
Dans **le camion**.
Dans le camion.
Dépêche-toi! *Dépêche-toi!*
Ding, ding, ding, ding.
Ding, ding, ding, ding.
Dépêche-toi! *Dépêche-toi!*
Monte à **l'échelle**!
Monte à l'échelle!
Dépêche-toi! *Dépêche-toi!*
Éteins **le feu**!
Éteins le feu!
Avec beaucoup **d'eau**.
Avec beaucoup d'eau.
Dépêche-toi! *Dépêche-toi!*

Hurry! *Hurry!*
Let's go! Let's go now!
Let's go! Let's go now!
In the **fire truck**.
In the fire truck.
Hurry! *Hurry!*
Ding, ding, ding, ding.
Ding, ding, ding, ding.
Hurry! *Hurry!*
Climb up the **ladder**!
Climb up the ladder!
Hurry! *Hurry!*
Put out the **fire**!
Put out the fire!
With a lot of **water**.
With a lot of water.
Hurry! *Hurry!*

Un feu de maison

Le camion de pompiers

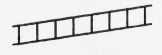

L'échelle

Le feu

Imaginons
Let's Imagine

Les princesses

Aimerais-tu être Blanche-Neige
   ou Cendrillon?
D'accord. Mets cette **couronne**.
Maintenant, nous avons besoin
   d'un chevalier.
Tu es le chevalier, d'accord?
Utilise le balai comme **cheval**.
Utilise la règle comme **épée**.
Le canapé est **le château**.
Monte sur le canapé.
Chevalier, sauve-nous!
Nous sommes prises au piège dans
   la tour!
Regarde, Cendrillon!
Là, je vois un chevalier.
Crions!
Ici, ici, chevalier!
Il nous a vues! Il nous a vues!
Regarde! Il a une épée! Il va
   nous sauver.

Princesses

Would you like to be Snow White
   or Cinderella?
Okay. Put on this **crown**.
Now, we need
   a **knight**.
You are the knight, okay?
Use the broom as a **horse**.
Use the ruler as a **sword**.
The sofa is the **castle**.
Get on the sofa.
Knight, save us!
We are trapped in
   the **tower**!
Look, Cinderella!
There, I see a knight.
Let's scream!
Here, here, knight!
He has seen us! He has seen us!
Look! He has a sword! He will
   save us.

Did You Know?

Long ago, France was a country of knights, castles, kings, queens, princes, and princesses. If you go to France, you will be able to visit magnificent castles all over the country, and especially along the Loire River. Be sure to visit also the palace of Versailles in the Paris area and the Louvre Museum in Paris, which was originally the castle of numerous kings and queens.

Une princesse

Une couronne

Un chevalier

Une épée

Les pirates

Pirates

Je suis **le pirate** Barbe-Bleue.
J'ai **la carte du trésor** caché.
Le trésor est sur **une île déserte**.
Regarde la carte.
Voilà **le vaisseau**. Tous à bord!
En avant! Allons-y!
Je suis **le capitaine**
parce que j'ai le chapeau le plus grand.
En avant! Allons-y!
Commence à ramer, **la tempête** arrive.
*Nous avons oublié de lever **l'ancre**.*
Quel vent! Aux voiles!
La Princesse Belle pleure
car elle est effrayée.
Elle veut un câlin et un bisou,
mais les pirates ne font pas de bisous.
D'accord, allez viens et rame.
Nous allons dans la mauvaise direction.
Tourne.
Terre! Terre!
Je vois l'île!

I am the **pirate** Blue Beard.
Here I have the hidden **treasure map**.
The treasure is on a **deserted island**.
Look at the map.
Here is the **ship**. All aboard!
Get moving! Quickly!
I am the **captain**
because I have the biggest hat.
Get moving! Let's go!
Start rowing, the **storm** is coming.
*We forgot to pull up the **anchor**.*
What a wind! To the sails!
Princess Belle is crying
because she's scared.
She wants a hug and a kiss,
but pirates don't give kisses.
Okay, then come on and row.
We are going in the wrong direction.
Let's turn around.
Land! Land!
I see the island!

Une carte

Un trésor

Les rames

L'ancre

Dans la voiture
In the Car

Au garage

At the Auto Mechanic

La voiture ne marche pas.	The **car** doesn't work.
Pouvez-vous m'aider?	Will you help me?
Réparons-la.	*Let's fix it.*
Elle fait un drôle de bruit au démarrage.	It makes a funny noise when it starts.
Écoutez: "Rrrrr poufff!"	Listen: "Rrrrr puff!"
Quel bruit étrange!	*What a strange noise!*
Regardons **le moteur**.	Let's look at the **engine**.
Passez-moi **la clef anglaise**, s'il vous plaît.	Pass me the **monkey wrench**, please.
C'est bon.	This is fine.
Passez-moi **le marteau**.	Pass me the **hammer**.
C'est bon.	This is fine.
Passez-moi **le tournevis**.	Pass me the **screwdriver**.
Ça n'est pas ça non plus.	This isn't it either.
Passez-moi **les pinces**.	Pass me the **pliers**.
Oh! Et qu'est-ce que c'est?	Oh! And what is this?
Je vais tirer. C'est un câble qui a lâché.	*I'm going to pull. It's a loose cable.*
Appliquons le plan deux.	Now for plan two.
Appelons un vrai mécanicien.	Let's call a real mechanic.

Did You Know?

Living in another country is like driving a car for the first time. The language is the key to the car, but you also need to know what to do with it. If you don't, chances are you will be stuck in the driver's seat with no idea of what to do next. You'll experience culture shock. A good language program offers both language and culture.

Une clef anglaise

Un marteau

Un tournevis

Les pinces

À la station-service

At the Gas Station

Jouons à **la station-service**.	Let's play **gas station**.
Mets ta **casquette**.	Put on your **cap**.
Le plein de super, s'il vous plaît.	Fill 'er up with super, please.
Carte ou *liquide*?	***Credit card*** or ***cash***?
Carte. Voilà.	Credit card. Here.
*Ouvrez **le réservoir**, s'il vous plaît.*	*Open the **tank**, please.*
Le tuyau est trop court.	The **hose** doesn't reach.
Déplacez la voiture.	*Move the car up.*
C'est bon, merci.	*That's enough, thanks.*
Nettoyons la voiture maintenant.	Now let's clean the car.
Remonte **les vitres**.	Roll up the **windows**.
J'apporte **le seau** et **les éponges**.	I'll bring the **bucket** and the **sponges**.
Essuie bien **les roues**. Avec plus de savon.	Wipe the **wheels** well. With more soap.
Enlève **la poussière** à l'intérieur.	Clean the **dust** inside.
Prends ce **chiffon**.	Take this **cloth**.
Essuie bien **le volant**.	Wipe the **steering wheel** well.
Maintenant passe **l'aspirateur** sur les sièges.	Now run the **vacuum cleaner** over the seats.
Rinçons la voiture.	Let's rinse the car.
Et maintenant séchons-la.	And now let's wipe it dry.

Une carte de crédit

De l'argent liquide

Une vitre de voiture

Un volant

Faire du sport
Playing Sports

Jouons au football

Joue au **football** avec
tes amis David et Sonia!
Nous avons besoin **d'un ballon** et
    d'un filet.
*David est **le gardien de but**.*
*Marquons **un but**.*
Allez, cours, fais une passe.
But! Buuuut!
Maintenant, tu es le gardien de but.
Va au filet.
Allez, Sonia, fais une passe!
Touche!
*Fais **un tir en corner**.*
Frappe avec ta tête.
Allez, cours, fais une passe.
Marquons un autre but!

Playing Soccer

Let's play **soccer** with
your friends David and Sonia!
We need a **ball** and
    a **net**.
*David is the **goalie**.*
*Let's score a **goal** on him.*
Come on, run, pass the ball.
Goal! Goooooooal!
Now, you are the goalie.
Go to the net.
Come on, Sonia, pass the ball!
Out of bounds!
*Make a **corner kick**.*
Hit it with your head.
Come on, run, pass the ball.
Let's score another goal!

Did You Know?

Jump rope is still a very popular game among girls in France. You can play alone or in a group. It is best to start with the two rope turners moving the rope from side to side while a third child jumps. The rope can also be moved in a whole circle.

Un ballon de football

Le filet

Le gardien de but

Touche!

Jouons à la corde à sauter

Let's Jump Rope

Sautons à **la corde**.
C'est ton tour. Un, deux et trois…
Le prénom de Marie
a cinq lettres,
M, A, R, I, E:
Ma-rie.
Le prénom de Camille a sept lettres,
C, A, M, I, L, L, E:
Ca-mil-le.
Maintenant **l'alphabet**.
A, B, C, D, E, F, G, H, I,
J, K, L, M, N, O, P,
Q, R, S, T, U, V, W, X, Y, Z.
Maintenant **les voyelles**.
A, E, I, O, U
A... **amour**
E... **écho**
I... **indien**
O... **ours**
U... **une**

Let's **jump rope**.
It's your turn. One, two, and three . . .
Marie's name
has five letters,
M, A, R, I, E:
Ma-rie.
Camille's name has seven letters,
C, A, M, I, L, L, E:
Ca-mil-le.
Now the **alphabet**.
A, B, C, D, E, F, G, H, I,
J, K, L, M, N, O, P,
Q, R, S, T, U, V, W, X, Y, Z.
Now the **vowels**.
A, E, I, O, U
A . . . **love**
E . . . **echo**
I . . . **Indian**
O . . .**bear**
U . . . **one**

Une corde à sauter

Un indien

Un ours

Un

En promenade

Going Places

Je vais faire du vélo

I Am Going on My Bicycle

Nous allons faire du vélo.	We are going to ride our bikes.
Mets ton **casque**—on y va!	Put on your **helmet**—and we go!
Nous allons dans **le parc**.	We are going through the **park**.
Il y a plein de gens.	There are lots of people.
Roulons doucement.	Let's go slowly.
Je fais du vélo. Je fais du vélo.	I'm riding my bike. I'm riding my bike.
Je fais du vélo dans le parc.	I'm riding my bike through the park.
Nous allons sur **la route**.	We are going on the **road**.
Allons vite.	Let's go quickly.
Je fais du vélo. Je fais du vélo.	I'm riding my bike. I'm riding my bike.
Je fais du vélo sur la route.	I'm riding my bike on the road.
Nous allons dans **la campagne**.	We are going through the **countryside**.
Il y a tellement de bosses!	There are so many bumps!
Je fais du vélo. Je fais du vélo.	I'm riding my bike. I'm riding my bike.
Je fais du vélo dans la campagne.	I'm riding my bike through the countryside.
Nous allons grimper la **montagne**.	We are going up the **mountain**.
Montons.	Let's go uphill.
Je fais du vélo. Je fais du vélo.	I'm riding my bike. I'm riding my bike.
Je monte avec mon vélo.	I'm riding my bike uphill.
Et maintenant je descends!	And now downhill!

Did You Know?

This is a great game to play indoors. Sit on the floor and start "pedaling." Jump up and down when hitting a "bump," stick your tongue out and pretend to be out of breath when "going uphill," and scream when "going downhill." You can make a "traffic light" with cardboard and green, yellow, and red cellophane paper. Use a flashlight to simulate turning the lights on and off.

Un casque

Une route

La campagne

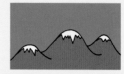
La montagne

Le feu tricolore

The Traffic Light

Rentre dans **la voiture**.
Attache ta **ceinture** et—on y va!
Regarde **le feu**.
Feu vert! Feu vert!
Qu'est-ce que je fais?
Je vais vite, vite, vite.
Biiip, biiip! Tuutt, tuutt!
Feu orange! Feu orange!
Qu'est-ce que je fais?
Je vais doucement, doucement,
    très doucement.
Feu rouge! Feu rouge!
Qu'est-ce que je fais?
Je m'arrête.

Get in the **car**.
Buckle your **belt**—and let's go!
Look at the **traffic light**.
Green light! Green light!
What do I do?
I go fast, fast, fast.
Beep, beep! Honk, honk!
Yellow light! Yellow light!
What do I do?
I go slowly, slowly,
    very slowly.
Red light! Red light!
What do I do?
I stop.

Une voiture

Le feu vert

Le feu orange

Le feu rouge

Allons au parc!
Let's Go to the Park!

Au parc

Nous sommes arrivés au **parc**.
Aimerais-tu aller sur **le toboggan**?
Allez, monte.
Un, deux, trois, quatre, cinq, six.
Très bien, assieds-toi maintenant.
Tiens-toi bien et descends!
Aimerais-tu aller aux **barres**?
Allez, monte.
Un, deux, trois, quatre, cinq, six.
Aimerais-tu aller dans **la tour**?
Allez, monte.
Un, deux, trois, quatre, cinq, six.

In the Park

We have arrived at the **park**.
Would you like to go on the **slide**?
Come on, go up.
One, two, three, four, five, six.
Very good, sit down now.
Hold on tight and go down!
Would you like to go to the **monkey bars**?
Come on, go up.
One, two, three, four, five, six.
Would you like to go to the **tower**?
Come on, go up.
One, two, three, four, five, six.

Did You Know?

Le goûter *is snack time in France. A snack is usually eaten by children after school between 4:30 and 5:00 P.M. This snack is generally some bread with butter and chocolate or cookies. Children drink hot chocolate, milk, or fruit juice.* Le goûter *is important in France because children are hungry when they leave school and dinnertime is far away.*

Un parc

Un toboggan

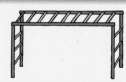

Les barres

Une tour

A la balançoire

On the Swings

Allons à **la balançoire**.	Let's go to the **swings**.
Veux-tu que je te pousse?	Shall I push you?
Et voilà!	There you go!
Plus fort!	*Harder!*
Pourquoi ne pousses-tu pas toi-même?	Why don't you push yourself?
Voyons, soulève tes jambes.	Let's see, pump your legs forward.
Maintenant abaisse tes jambes.	Now pump your legs back.
Comme ça, en avant, en arrière.	Like that, forward, back.
En avant, en arrière.	*Forward, back.*
Veux-tu arrêter?	Do you want to stop?
Allons à **la bascule**.	Let's go to the **seesaw**.
C'est occupé. Nous allons attendre.	It's full. We'll have to wait.
As-tu faim?	Are you hungry?
Oui, je t'ai apporté	Yes, I brought you
un sandwich au jambon.	a **ham sandwich**.

Une balançoire

Une bascule

Un sandwich

Le jambon

Allons nous amuser!

Let's Go to Fun Places!

Au zoo

Nous sommes au **zoo**. Nous sommes au zoo.

Je vois les lions. Nous sommes au zoo.

Le lion fait, "Grrrr".

Le lion dort.

La lionne est là-bas.

Le lion a **une crinière** et la lionne n'en a pas.

Les girafes sont là-bas.

Comme elles ont un grand **cou**!

Leurs **jambes** sont très longues, aussi.

Les éléphants sont là-bas.

Comme ils ont de grandes **oreilles**!

Regarde comment ils attrapent les cacahuètes avec leur **trompe**.

Regarde, les tigres.

Comme ils ont une grande **gueule**!

Regarde, **les ours**!

Ils sont très grands.

Regarde, voilà les **serpents**.

Les serpents font, "Ssss".

Ils sont très longs.

At the Zoo

We are in the **zoo**. We are in the zoo.

I see the lions. We are in the zoo.

The lion says, "Grrrrr."

The **lion** is sleeping.

The **lioness** is over there.

The lion has a **mane** and the lioness doesn't.

*The **giraffes** are over there.*

What long **necks** they have!

Their **legs** are very long, too.

*The **elephants** are over there.*

What big **ears** they have!

Look how they get the peanuts with their **trunk**.

*Look, the **tigers**.*

What large **mouths** they have!

Look, the **bears**!

They are very big.

Look, here are the **snakes**.

The snakes say, "Ssss."

They are very long.

Did You Know?

French is spoken not only in France, but in many other places as well: in Belgium, Switzerland, Monaco, Canada, in more than twenty African countries, in Martinique, Guadeloupe, Haiti, French Guyana, and Polynesia. From one region to another, there are different accents and vocabulary, but French-speakers always manage to understand one another.

Un lion et une lionne

Une girafe

Un éléphant

Un tigre

Au parc d'attractions

At the Amusement Park

Allons acheter **les billets**.	Let's buy the **tickets**.
À quel manège veux-tu aller?	Which ride do you want to go on?
*À **la grande roue**.*	*On the **Ferris wheel**.*
Asseyons-nous. Assieds-toi là.	Let's sit down. Sit here.
Donne le ticket à la dame.	Give the ticket to the lady.
Ouah! Comme c'est haut!	*Wow! How high!*
Aimerais-tu aller au **carrousel**?	Would you like to go on the **merry-go-round**?
Je te mets sur **le cheval**. Hop!	I'll get you up on the **horse**. Up!
Tiens-toi bien. Comme ça.	Hold on tight. Like this.
Je vais te tenir, ne t'inquiète pas.	I will hold you, don't worry.
Donne le ticket au monsieur.	Give the ticket to the man.
Où aimerais-tu aller maintenant?	Where would you like to go now?
*Aux **autos-tamponneuses**.*	*To the **bumper cars**.*
Cours, allons dans la voiture rouge. Monte.	Run, let's go to the red car. Get in.
Je viens avec toi, ne t'inquiète pas.	I'll go with you, don't worry.
Tu conduis.	You drive.
*Aux **montagnes russes**.*	*The **roller coaster**.*
Nous ferons cela quand tu seras plus grand!	We'll do that when you are older!

La grande roue

Un carrousel

Les autos-tamponneuses

Les montagnes russes

39

Allons au musée!

Let's Go to the Museum!

Au musée de sciences naturelles

In the Museum of Natural Science

Viens, je crois que **les dinosaures**
sont dans cette salle.
*C'est **un tyrannosaure**.*
C'est immense!
Les tyrannosaures mangeaient
les autres dinosaures.
Ils étaient **carnivores**.
Ils avaient **des dents** très pointues.
Regarde, **une empreinte de pied de
 brachiosaure**.
C'est gigantesque!
Les brachiosaures étaient énormes,
mais ils mangeaient
 des feuilles d'arbres.
Ils étaient **herbivores**.
Regarde, c'est un **stégosaure**.
Les stégosaures avaient
une très petite tête.

Come, I think the **dinosaurs**
are in this room.
*It's a **tyrannosaurus**.*
It's huge!
Tyrannosauruses ate
other dinosaurs.
They were **carnivores**.
They had very sharp **teeth**.
Look, a **brachiosaurus
 footprint**.
It's gigantic!
Brachiosauruses were enormous,
but they ate
 tree leaves.
They were **herbivores**.
Look, it's a **stegosaurus**.
Stegosauruses had
very small heads.

Did You Know?

*Located in the heart of Paris, the Musée d'Histoire Naturelle is a wonderful place for adults
and children to visit. Walking through the dinosaur gallery is a great way to get an idea of what
life was like in prehistoric times. After your visit to the dinosaur gallery, you can also take a
walk through the Jardin des Plantes, where you will find exhibits of living spiders and snakes!*

Un tyrannosaure

Une empreinte de pied

Un brachiosaure

Un stégosaure

Au musée d'art

At the Art Museum

Allons voir la salle Dali.
Dali était un peintre espagnol.
*Regarde ce **tableau**.*
Il y a trois visages cachés.
Peux-tu les voir?
Regarde attentivement.
    Vois-tu les visages?
Il y a un enfant, une jeune personne
et une personne âgée.
"Les Trois Ages".
Viens par là.
C'est **une sculpture** de
    Fernando Botero,
un sculpteur et **peintre** colombien.
Regarde, ils ont un atelier de peinture.
Prends **un pinceau**.
Mets **un tablier**.
    Attends, je vais t'attacher.
Maintenant **les peintures**.
Laquelle veux-tu?
Que vas-tu peindre?
Mets un peu de peinture sur **la palette**.
Maintenant touche la peinture
    avec le pinceau.

Let's go to see Dali's hall.
Dali was a Spanish artist.
*Look at this **painting**.*
There are three hidden faces.
Can you see them?
Look closely.
    Do you see the faces?
They are a child, a young person,
and an old person.
"The Three Ages."
Come this way.
This is a **sculpture** by
    Fernando Botero,
a Colombian sculptor and **painter**.
Look, they have a painting workshop.
Get a **brush**.
Put on a **robe**.
    Wait, I'll tie you.
Now the **paints**.
Which ones do you want?
What are you going to paint?
Put a little bit of paint on the **palette**.
Now touch the paint
    with the brush.

Un tableau

Une sculpture

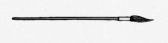

Un pinceau

Une palette

Visite à la famille
Visiting Family

On va chez Grand-père et Grand-mère

Going to Grandma and Grandpa's

Nous allons chez **Grand-mère et Grand-père**.

C'est leur **anniversaire de mariage**.

Nous allons manger **des crêpes**.

C'est délicieux!

Tante Simone et **Oncle** Antoine seront là,

et également ta **cousine** préférée Isabelle.

Mais tu devras jouer aussi avec ton **cousin** Jean.

Nous sommes arrivés! Sors de la voiture.

Salue tout le monde.

Donne un baiser à ta grand-mère et fais-lui un câlin.

Joyeux anniversaire de mariage!

We are going to **grandma and grandpa's** house.

It's their **anniversary**.

We are going to eat **crêpes**.

How delicious!

Aunt Simone and **Uncle** Antoine will be there,

and also your favorite **cousin**, Isabel.

But you will have to play with your **cousin** Jean as well.

We arrived! Get out of the car.

Greet everybody.

Give your grandma a kiss and a hug.

Happy anniversary!

Did You Know?

Crêpes are a kind of paper-thin pancake, very well known and much appreciated in France. They are made with wheat flour or sometimes with buckwheat flour (dinner crêpes), eggs, and milk. After cooking, dessert crêpes can be topped with sugar, fruit, chocolate, or any number of other choices. Dinner crêpes can be topped with anything from ham, cheese, and eggs to seafood. Crêpes are enjoyed throughout France, but they are the specialty of La Bretagne, which is located in the northwest part of France.

Le grand-père et la grand-mère

L'oncle et la tante

Les cousins

Le père et la mère

Ma famille

My Family

J'ai **une grand-mère**	I have a **grandmother**
dont le nom est Joséphine.	whose name is Josephine.
Quand elle **est contente**,	When she **is happy**,
elle passe son temps dans la cuisine.	she spends her time in the kitchen.
J'ai **un grand-père**	I have a **grandfather**
dont le nom est Étienne.	whose name is Steve.
Quand il **est fâché**,	When he **is angry**,
il passe son temps dans le jardin.	he spends his time in the garden.
J'ai **une tante**	I have an **aunt**
dont le nom est Nicole.	whose name is Nicole.
Quand elle **est fatiguée**,	When she **is tired**,
elle passe son temps dans la maison.	she spends her time in the house.
J'ai **un oncle**	I have an **uncle**
dont le nom est Joseph.	whose name is Joseph.
Quand il **est triste**,	When he **is sad**,
il passe son temps au café.	he spends his time in the coffee shop.
J'ai **une sœur**	I have a **sister**
dont le nom est Suzanne.	whose name is Susan.
Quand elle **s'ennuie**,	When she **is bored**,
elle passe son temps près de la fenêtre.	she spends her time at the window.
Oh, ah! Et j'ai aussi	Uh, oh! And I also have
mon **père** et ma **mère**.	my **father** and my **mother**.

Je suis content/e.

Je suis fatigué/e.

Je suis triste.

Je m'ennuie.

Les animaux
Animals

Les animaux jouent The Animals Play

Les petits oiseaux qui volent dans l'air
volent, volent, volent, volent, volent.
Les petits poissons qui nagent
    dans l'eau
nagent, nagent, nagent, nagent, nagent.
Les uns et les autres sous le soleil,
les uns et les autres jouent comme moi.
Les petits chevaux qui galopent dans
    la montagne
galopent, galopent, galopent, galopent,
    galopent.
Les petits lapins qui sautent dans
    le champ
sautent, sautent, sautent, sautent,
    sautent.
Les uns et les autres sous le soleil,
les uns et les autres jouent comme moi.
Les petits serpents qui rampent sur
    le sol
rampent, rampent, rampent, rampent,
    rampent.
Les petits écureuils qui grimpent
    aux arbres
grimpent, grimpent, grimpent,
    grimpent, grimpent.
Les uns et les autres sous le soleil,
les uns et les autres jouent comme moi.

The **little birds** that fly in the air
fly, fly, fly, fly, fly.
The **little fish** that swim
    in the water
swim, swim, swim, swim, swim.
These and those under the sun,
these and those play like me.
The **little horses** that gallop in
    the mountains
gallop, gallop, gallop, gallop,
    gallop.
The **little rabbits** that jump in
    the field
jump, jump, jump, jump,
    jump.
These and those under the sun,
these and those play like me.
The **little snakes** that slither on
    the ground
slither, slither, slither, slither,
    slither.
The **little squirrels** that climb in
    the trees
climb, climb, climb,
climb, climb.
These and those under the sun,
these and those play like me.

Un oiseau

Un poisson

Un lapin

Un écureuil

À la ferme

At the Farm

Nous sommes arrivés à **la ferme**.
Voilà **les poules**.
Les poules font, "Cot, cot, cot".
Voilà **les dindes**.
Les dindes font, "Glou, glou, glou".
Regarde, **le coq** est monté sur le toit.
Le coq fait, "Cocorico!"
Aimerais-tu jeter des miettes aux
    poussins?
Les poussins font: "Puiii, puiii, puiiii".
Allons voir **les chevaux**.
Le poulain est avec sa mère,
    la jument.
Le cheval est le père.
Tu veux voir **les vaches**?
Le taureau est le père,
la vache est la mère
et **le veau** est le bébé.
Regarde, le petit veau est
    en train de têter.
Il boit du lait de sa maman.

We have arrived at the **farm**.
Here are the **hens**.
The hens say, "Cluck, cluck, cluck."
Here are the **turkeys**.
The turkeys say, "Gobble, gobble, gobble."
Look, the **rooster** is up on the roof.
The rooster says, "Cock-a-doodle-doo!"
Would you like to throw crumbs to the
    chicks?
The chicks say, "Peep, peep, peep."
Let's go see the **horses**.
The **foal** is with his mom,
    the **mare**.
The **stallion** is the dad.
You want to see the **cows**?
The **bull** is the dad,
the **cow** is the mom,
and the **calf** is the baby.
Look, the little calf is
    nursing.
He's drinking milk from his mom.

Une ferme

Une poule

Un cheval

Une vache

Je ne me sens pas bien
I Don't Feel Well

Chez le docteur

To the Doctor's

Oh! Quelle **toux**!

Dis-moi, où as tu mal?

Est-ce que tu as mal à **la gorge**?

Ouvre grand ta bouche, plus grand.

Fais ahhhhhh très fort.

Très bien!

Ta gorge est enflammée.

Est-ce que tu as mal aux oreilles?

Laisse-moi voir cette **oreille**.

Cette oreille va bien. Regardons celle-là.

Celle-ci est infectée!

Quel **nez congestionné**!

Tiens, **un mouchoir**.

Mouche ton **nez**.

Quel **rhume** tu as!

Mets **le thermomètre**.

Tu as de **la fièvre**.

Prends **une cuillère à soupe**
    de ce **sirop**

deux fois par jour.

Bois beaucoup d'eau.

Reviens dans une semaine.

Porte-toi mieux!

Oh! What a **cough**!

Tell me, what hurts?

Does your **throat** hurt?

Open your mouth wide, wider.

Say ahhhhhh very loud.

Very good!

Your throat is inflamed.

Do your ears hurt?

Let me see this **ear**.

This ear is okay. Let's see this one.

This one is infected!

What a **runny nose**!

Here, a **tissue**.

Blow your **nose**.

What a **cold** you have!

Put in the **thermometer**.

You have a **fever**.

Take a **tablespoon**
    of this **syrup**

two times a day.

Drink a lot of water.

Come back in a week.

Get well!

Did You Know?

Different languages reflect different cultures and different ways of understanding daily life. That is why literal translations can sometimes be linguistically correct but culturally entirely inappropriate. Learning a language is very useful but it is very important to know the culture as well.

Une gorge enflammée

Une oreille

Un nez congestionné

Un nez rouge

Le rhume

Tôt ce matin,
le garçon s'est réveillé,
avec un **mal de gorge**
et une grosse toux.
Euf, euf, euf, euf.
Aïe! Pauvre petit garçon!
Quel rhume il a!
Il a éternué à nouveau.
Atchoum, atchoum, atchoum!
Ses **yeux** larmoient,
son nez le démange.
Sa mère lui apporte
un sirop gris.
Atchoum, atchoum, atchoum!
Aïe! Pauvre petit garçon!
Quel rhume il a!
Il a éternué à nouveau.
Atchoum, atchoum,
    atchoum!

The Cold

Early this morning,
the boy got up,
with a **sore throat**
and a big cough.
Cough, cough, cough, cough.
Ay! Poor little boy!
What a cold he has!
He sneezed again.
Achoo, achoo, achoo!
His **eyes** are watering,
his nose is itchy.
His mother brings him
a gray syrup.
Achoo, achoo, achoo!
Ay! Poor little boy!
What a cold he has!
He sneezed again.
Achoo, achoo,
    achoo!

Un thermomètre

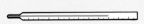

Une cuillère à soupe
de sirop

Le sirop

Les yeux larmoyants

Joyeux anniversaire!

Happy Birthday!

La fête d'anniversaire

The Birthday Party

Quel âge as-tu?	How old are you?
Six ans? Tu es un adulte.	Six? You are a grown-up.
Donne-moi ton oreille. Un, deux, trois, quatre,	Give me your ear. One, two, three, four,
cinq et six.	five, and six.
Et quel âge as-tu?	And how old are you?
Sept ans et demi?	Seven-and-a-half?
Tu es si vieux!	You are so old!
Prends tes **cadeaux**. Ouvre-les.	Take your **gifts**. Open them.
Allez, ouvre-les!	Come on, open them!
*C'est **un hélicoptère**!*	*It's a **helicopter**!*
Et celui-là aussi! Ouvre-le.	And this too! Open it.
Voyons. Qu'est-ce que c'est?	Let's see. What is it?
*C'est **un bateau de pirates**.*	*It's a **pirate boat**.*
Les enfants! Le gâteau!	Kids! The cake!

Did You Know?

The French word for birthday is anniversaire. *In English, the word* anniversary *is used for the celebration of marriage anniversaries. It is easy to understand how these terms are related, since their root refers to once a year. The term for a wedding anniversary in French is more precise. It is* anniversaire de mariage.

Un cadeau

Un hélicoptère

Un bateau

Un pirate

Le gâteau

Le gâteau arrive! Le gâteau!
Le gâteau arrive!
Venez tous!
Asseyez-vous ici.
Les lumières!
Éteignez les lumières, s'il vous plaît!
Chantons. Un, deux et trois.
Joyeux anniversaire,
  joyeux anniversaire,
nous te souhaitons tous
  un joyeux anniversaire.
Fais **un vœu**.
Souffle **les bougies**.
Souffle plus fort.
Bien! Qui veut du gâteau?
En veux-tu? Oui?
C'est un gâteau au chocolat!
Aimerais-tu **un gros** ou
  un petit morceau?

The Cake

The **cake** is coming! Cake!
The cake is coming!
Everybody, come!
Sit here.
Lights!
Turn off the lights, please!
Let's sing. One, two, and three.
Happy birthday to you,
  happy birthday to you,
we all wish you
  a happy birthday.
Make a **wish**.
Blow out the **candles**.
Blow harder.
Good! Who wants cake?
Do you want some? Yes?
It's a chocolate cake!
Would you like a **big** or
  small piece?

Un gâteau

Des bougie

Un gros morceau
de gâteau

Un petit morceau
de gâteau

Allons à la plage!
Let's Go to the Beach!

À la plage

Le **sable** est brûlant!

N'enlève pas tes **sandales**.

Prends **la serviette** dans ton **sac à dos**.

Étends-la sur le sable.

Viens, je vais te mettre
un peu de **crème solaire**.

Je ne veux pas que tu attrapes
des coups de soleil.

Un petit peu sur ton visage.

Maintenant sur tes bras et sur tes
jambes.

Les petits doigts de pied.

Attends! Ne t'en vas pas. Viens là!

Mets ta **casquette**, le soleil tape
très fort.

Aide-moi à faire un trou pour
le parasol.

Est-ce que je peux emprunter ta pelle?

Je creuse, je creuse, je creuse.

Et maintenant, à l'eau!

Mets ta **bouée**.

At the Beach

The **sand** is hot!

Don't take off your **sandals**.

Take the **towel** from your **backpack**.

Spread it on the sand.

Come here, I'll put
some **sunscreen** on you.

I don't want you to get
burned.

A little bit on your face.

Now on your arms and on your
legs.

Your little toes.

Wait! Don't go away. Come here!

Put on your **cap**, the sun is
very strong.

Help me make a hole for
the **umbrella**.

Can I borrow your shovel?

I am digging, digging, digging.

And now, to the water!

Put on your **inner tube**.

Did You Know?

*You can set up a "beach" in the playroom or the backyard.
Make a sun with construction paper. Mark off a pretend
swimming area with tape. You can make a sandbox with a large
container filled with sand and toys. Use a beach bag with
beach towels, sand toys, and sunscreen. Have fun!*

Les sandales

La crème solaire

Le parasol

La bouée

Les châteaux de sable

Sand Castles

Faisons **un château de sable**.	Let's make a **sand castle**.
Voilà **le seau**.	Here is the **bucket**.
Voilà **la pelle**.	Here is the **shovel**.
Remplis le seau avec du sable.	Fill the bucket with sand.
Maintenant renverse-le.	Now flip it over.
Tapote doucement.	Pat it softly.
Pain dur, se ramollit.	*Hard bread, soften up.*
Pain dur, se ramollit.	*Hard bread, soften up.*
Pain dur, se ramollit.	*Hard bread, soften up.*
Maintenant soulève le seau. Doucement!	Now lift the bucket. Slowly!
Comme c'est beau!	*How beautiful!*
Choisis **un moule** pour construire la tour.	Choose a **mold** to build a tower.
Remplis-le avec du sable.	Fill it with sand.
Renverse-le très doucement.	Flip it very slowly.
Prends **le rateau** et fais un chemin.	Take the **rake** and make a path.
Maintenant ramollis-le avec la main.	Now smooth it with your hand.
Prends la pelle et creuse **un fossé**.	Take the shovel and dig a **moat**.
Ne jette pas de sable!	Don't throw sand!
Regarde! Là tu as **des coquillages** et **des cailloux**	Look! Here you have **shells** and **stones**
pour décorer le château.	to decorate the castle.
Quel beau château!	*What a beautiful castle!*

Un château de sable

Un seau

La pelle

Un rateau

Au printemps
In the Spring

Mouvements du printemps

L'escargot, l'escargot
avance très lentement.
Avance lentement comme un escargot.
Le papillon, le papillon
volète parmi les fleurs.
Volète parmi les fleurs comme
le papillon.
La grenouille, la grenouille
saute dans l'eau.
Saute dans l'eau comme la grenouille.
La coccinelle, la coccinelle
est très petite.
Tu es petit/e comme la coccinelle.
Le vent, le vent
souffle et souffle.
Souffle comme le vent.
La fleur, la fleur
ondule dans le vent.
Ondule comme la fleur.
Le printemps est là!

Spring's Movements

The snail, the snail
moves very slowly.
Move slowly like the snail.
The butterfly, the butterfly
flutters among the flowers.
Flutter among the flowers like
the butterfly.
The frog, the frog
jumps in the water.
Jump in the water like the frog.
The ladybug, the ladybug
is very small.
You are small like the ladybug.
The wind, the wind
blows and blows.
Blow like the wind.
The flower, the flower
waves in the wind.
Wave like a flower.
Spring is here!

Did You Know?

"Il pleut bergère" is a classic French song for young children. In the past, families would choose a little boy or girl who would be in charge of caring for the sheep on the farm. Though this tradition doesn't exist anymore, the song is still sung and enjoyed by children and their parents as well.

Un escargot

Un papillon

Une grenouille

Une coccinelle

La pluie

Il pleut! Mets tes **bottes**.
Maintenant **l'imperméable**.
Ouvrons **les parapluies**.
Quelle pluie! C'est **une averse**!
    Chantons!
Il pleut, il pleut, bergère,
Presse tes blancs moutons.
Allons à ma chaumière,
Bergère, vite allons.
J'entends sur le feuillage
l'eau qui tombe à grand bruit.
Voici, venir l'orage.
Voici, l'éclair qui luit.
Sautons dans **la flaque d'eau**!
La pluie s'est arrêtée. *Ça sent si bon!*
C'est l'odeur du printemps.

The Rain

It's raining! Put on your **boots**.
Now the **raincoat**.
Let's open the **umbrellas**.
What a rain! It's a **downpour**!
    Let's sing!
It's raining, it's raining, shepherdess,
Hurry along your white sheep.
Come to my cottage,
Shepherdess, let's go quickly now.
I hear the sound of the heavy
rain falling on the leaves.
See, the storm is coming.
See, the lightning is lurking.
Let's jump in the **puddle**!
It stopped raining. *It smells so good!*
It's the smell of spring.

Les bottes

L'imperméable

Le parapluie

Une averse

En été
In the Summer

Allons pêcher

Shuuut! Silence!
Nous allons voir s'il y a du poisson.
Jette du pain. Comme ça, plus de
    miettes.
Il y a beaucoup de poissons.
Prends ta **canne à pêche**.
Accroche **l'appât** à **l'hameçon**.
Lance ta **ligne**. Très bien.
Attendons.
Quelque chose a mordu!
Tiens bien ta canne et tire. Tire!
*C'est **une botte**. Beurk!*
Mets plus **d'appât** et lance la ligne.
Quelque chose a mordu!
Tiens bien ta canne et tire. Tire!
*Ouah! C'est **un poisson géant**.*
Ça doit être **le roi des poissons**.
Mets-le dans **le panier**.
Mets plus d'appât et lance ta ligne.
Quelque chose a mordu!
C'est une boîte de conserve. Beurk!
Au moins c'est **une boîte de sardines**!

Let's Go Fishing

Shhhh! Silence!
We are going to see if there are fish.
Throw bread. Like this, more
    crumbs.
There are many fish.
Take your **fishing pole**.
Put the **bait** on the **hook**.
Cast the **line**. Great.
Let's wait.
Something bit!
Hold your pole tight and pull. Pull!
*It's a **boot**. Yikes!*
Put on more **bait** and cast the line.
Something bit!
Hold your pole tight and pull. Pull!
*Wow! It's a **giant fish**.*
It must be the **king of fish**.
Put it in the **basket**.
Put on more bait and cast the line.
Something bit!
It's a can. Yikes!
At least it's a **can of sardines**!

Did You Know?

*Throw a blue tablecloth on the floor and use a large box or a coffee table placed upside
down as a boat. For the fishing activity, place a few objects in the "river" and try to fish
them out with a pole made with a stick and cord. (You may want to attach magnets
to the pole and the objects you're fishing for.) Show a picture or a puppet of a wave,
crocodile, and waterfall for the song.*

Une canne à pêche

Un hameçon

Un poisson géant

Une boîte de sardines

Sur la rivière

By the River

Note: After each verse, repeat the *refrain*/chorus.

Refrain:
Dans mon **bateau** je rame.
Sur la rivière je vais,
sur la rivière je vais, sur la rivière je vais.

Une vague géante arrive!
Une vague arrive! Une vague arrive!
Couvre ton nez!
Une vague arrive là.
Bonne nouvelle elle s'en va. *(Refrain)*

Un crocodile arrive!
Rame vite, rame vite!
Un crocodile arrive! Un crocodile arrive!
Un crocodile arrive là.
Bonne nouvelle il s'en va. *(Refrain)*

Une cascade arrive!
Qu'allons-nous faire, qu'allons-nous
    faire?
Une cascade arrive!
Une cascade arrive là.
Bonne nouvelle elle s'en va. *(Refrain)*

Chorus:
In my **boat** I row.
By the river I go,
by the river I go, by the river I go.

A huge **wave** is coming!
The wave is coming! The wave is coming!
Cover your nose!
A wave is coming here.
Good thing it's going away. *(Chorus)*

A **crocodile** is coming!
Row fast, row fast!
A crocodile is coming! A crocodile is coming!
A crocodile is coming here.
Good thing it's going away. *(Chorus)*

A **waterfall** is coming!
What do we do, what do we
    do?
A waterfall is coming!
A waterfall is coming here.
Good thing it's going away. *(Chorus)*

Un bateau

Une vague

Un crocodile   Une cascade

En automne

In the Fall

Les squelettes

The Skeletons

Note: After each hour, repeat the *refrain*/chorus "Tomb, tomb, tomba-la-ca-tomb, tomb, tomb, tomba-la-ca-tomb."

Quand **l'horloge** sonne une heure, **les squelettes** sortent de leurs tombes.	When the **clock** strikes one, the **skeletons** get out of their tombs.
Quand l'horloge sonne deux heures, Les squelettes regardent **l'horloge**.	When the clock strikes two, the skeletons look at the **clock**.
Quand l'horloge sonne trois heures, les squelettes touchent leurs **pieds**.	When the clock strikes three, the skeletons touch their **feet**.
Quand l'horloge sonne quatre heures, les squelettes cirent leurs **chaussures**.	When the clock strikes four, the skeletons polish their **shoes**.
Quand l'horloge sonne cinq heures, les squelettes font **du tricycle**.	When the clock strikes five, the skeletons ride their **tricycles**.
Quand l'horloge sonne six heures, les squelettes prennent **le train**.	When the clock strikes six, the skeletons ride on a **train**.
Quand l'horloge sonne sept heures, les squelettes font de **la trottinette**.	When the clock strikes seven, the skeletons ride on **scooters**.
Quand l'horloge sonne huit heures, les squelettes montent à **moto**.	When the clock strikes eight, the skeletons ride on their **motorcycles**.
Quand l'horloge sonne neuf heures, les squelettes **ne bougent pas**.	When the clock strikes nine, the skeletons **don't move**.
Quand l'horloge sonne dix heures, les squelettes **ne peuvent être vus**.	When the clock strikes ten, the skeletons **can't be seen**.
Quand l'horloge sonne onze heures, les squelettes **ne peuvent être entendus**.	When the clock strikes eleven, the skeletons **can't be heard**.
Quand l'horloge sonne douze heures, les squelettes ronflent dans **la nuit**.	When the clock strikes twelve, the skeletons snore in the **night**.

Un squelette

Un tricycle

Un train

Une trottinette

Une méchante sorcière

A Bad Witch

Une vilaine **sorcière** marche
    derrière nous.
Ferme bien les yeux.
Ouvre-les, tu verras!
Cours, cours! Attrape la sorcière!
Bravo! Tu l'as attrapée!
Un vilain **magicien** marche derrière nous.
Ferme bien les yeux.
Ouvre-les, tu verras!
Cours, cours! Attrape le magicien!
Bravo! Tu l'as attrapé!
Un vilain **fantôme** marche derrière nous.
Ferme bien les yeux.
Ouvre-les, tu verras!
Cours, cours! Attrape le fantôme!
Bravo! Tu l'as attrapé!
Un vilain **monstre** marche derrière nous.
Ferme bien les yeux.
Ouvre-les, tu verras!
Cours, cours! Attrape le monstre!
Bravo! Tu l'as attrapé!

A bad **witch** is walking
    behind us.
Close your eyes tight.
Open them, you'll see!
Run, run! Catch the witch!
Great! You caught her!
A bad **wizard** is walking behind us.
Close your eyes tight.
Open them, you'll see!
Run, run! Catch the wizard!
Great! You caught him!
A bad **ghost** is walking behind us.
Close your eyes tight.
Open them, you'll see!
Run, run! Catch the ghost!
Great! You caught him!
A bad **monster** is walking behind us.
Close your eyes tight.
Open them, you'll see!
Run, run! Catch the monster!
Great! You caught him!

Une moto

Une sorcière

Un fantôme

Un monstre

La tempête de neige

The Snowstorm

Il fait très froid.	It is very cold.
Oh! Comme il fait froid!	*Oh! How cold it is!*
Si f-f-f-roid!	How c-c-c-old!
J'ai très froid.	I am very cold.
Et toi? As-tu froid?	What about you? Are you cold?
J'ai très froid.	*I am very cold.*
Regarde, il neige.	Look, it is snowing.
Comme c'est beau!	*How beautiful!*
Il neige! *Merveilleux!*	It is snowing! *Great!*
Touche **la neige**.	Touch the **snow**.
Comme la neige est froide!	How cold is the snow!
Ouh! Comme c'est froid!	*Uy! How cold it is!*
Si f-f-f-roid!	How c-c-c-old!
Faisons **des boules de neige**.	Let's make some **snowballs**.
Prends un peu de neige. *Comme ça.*	Get some snow. *Like this.*
Fais une boule. *Comme ça.*	Make a ball. *Like this.*
Un, deux, trois…	One, two, three . . .
Lance-la!	Throw it!
Aïe!	Hey!
Je t'ai eu!	Got you!

Did You Know?

In the winter months, the French love to ski. Often, they go skiing in Les Alpes, *mountains located in the southeast of France and in the bordering countries of Switzerland and Italy, or in* Le Jura, *the natural border between France and Switzerland, or even in* Les Pyrénées, *which separate France from Spain.*

Une tempête de neige

Une grosse boule

Une boule moyenne

Une petite boule

Le bonhomme de neige

The Snowman

Note: Repeat the *refrain*/chorus after each verse.

Refrain:
Je suis **un bonhomme de neige**
et je danse mieux en hiver.

Une grosse boule!
Une boule moyenne!
Et une petite boule!
Pour la tête. *(Refrain)*

Je bouge *mes **bras*** comme ça!
Je bouge *mes **pieds*** comme ça!
Je bouge *mon **chapeau*** comme ça!
Un, deux, trois. *(Refrain)*

Oh, non! Le soleil est apparu!
Il fait si chaud, si chaud, si chaud!
Je fonds! Je fonds!
Je suis **une petite flaque d'eau**.
Éclabousse-moi: splatch, splatch,
   splatch. *(Refrain)*

Chorus:
I am a **snowman**
and I dance better in winter.

*A **big ball**!*
*A **medium-sized ball**!*
*And a **small ball**!*
For the head. *(Chorus)*

I move *my **arms*** like this!
I move *my **feet*** like this!
I move *my **hat*** like this!
One, two, three. *(Chorus)*

Oh, no! The sun came out!
It is so hot, so hot, so hot!
I am melting! I am melting!
I am a **little puddle of water**.
Splash in me: splash, splash,
   splash. *(Chorus)*

Les bras

Les pieds

Un chapeau

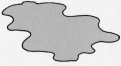
Une flaque d'eau

About the Authors

Ana Lomba is the founder and director of Sueños de Colores LLC, a company offering online language learning instruction and resources for preschools and families of children up to seven years old. Nominated "Best of the Conference 2002" at the Foreign Language Educators of New Jersey annual conference, Ana was a featured speaker at the Northeast Conference on the Teaching of Foreign Languages in April 2003. She is presently the Early Childhood Contributing Editor of *Learning Languages: The Journal of the National Network for Early Language Learning.* A native of Madrid, Spain, Ana currently lives with her husband and three kids in Princeton, New Jersey.

Marcela Summerville is the founder and director of Spanish Workshop for Children, an early language-learning program for preschools and children from birth to seven years old. A native of Puerto Madryn, Argentina, Marcela currently lives with her husband and two kids in Philadelphia, Pennsylvania.

Frank D. Jacobs